BLIZZARDS, SWORDS & TEARS

LAÒN

Blizzards, Swords & Tears

It is weakness not daring to talk about one's weaknesses.

It is strength to dare talk about one's lack of strength.

 **EYEWEAR** PUBLISHING

POETRY

First published in 2019
by Eyewear Publishing Ltd
Suite 333, 19-21 Crawford Street
Marylebone, London W1H 1PJ
United Kingdom

Cover design and typeset by Edwin Smet

Printed in England by TJ International Ltd, Padstow, Cornwall

ISBN 978-1-912477-74-6

WWW.EYEWEARPUBLISHING.COM

LAÒN,
a pseudonym for
Laura Amalie Ohmann Nielsen, was born in 1997
in a suburban town outside central Copenhagen, Denmark.
As the youngest child of four she grew up learning from her
older siblings' experiences; yet on her own she did learn
the current ways of the world. Writing became an escape,
and way of exploring. It became clear to her that love
and pain (in both sexual and mental life) are terrifyingly
important to write about.

TABLE OF CONTENTS

TEARS

To you who might need to know:
You are not the only one, and neither are
you alone although the fear of speaking up might
create such a feeling. May my words speak for
those who at this present moment
feel they cannot.

HOPE FOR CHANGE

An acknowledgment for the desired resolution

Writing to see it more clearly,
Hope for change.

Inspired by the early progress,
A different intent,
Declaring it growth.

Let the children once see clearly
The individuality of man.

After all, it is only natural for the lucky
To grow up uneven.

Blizzards

ACCEPTABLE

Sometimes I feel like I am broken. My chest ripped open, my mind torn apart.
Sometimes I feel like I am ruined. My heart shattered from your doing, my thoughts in wild cart.
I fear I am like the one before me, the one who was me before me.
I know you tell me I am not, but it does not take away my fears.
Because my fears are not necessarily rational. Not necessarily reasonable, clever.
But they are here, and they are mine. My fears. And that makes them suitable.

Sometimes I fear that I was blind before, that I did not see what was going on.
Sometimes I fear that I am pretending. That my soul was not scarred from this hurting, am I a con?
I know you tell me that nothing ever was wrong, but it does not take away my fears that it was.
Because my fears are not necessarily sensible. Not necessarily reachable, nor worthy to dissever.
But they are here, and they are mine. My fears. And that makes them acceptable.

Sometimes I fear I have gotten the worst from each one of you.
The mild covered by the rage, the earthbound covered by the fleeting.
I know you always tell me you are proud of me, for everything I have achieved.
Still my mind, heart and soul are still bleeding.
And that is suitable, that is acceptable.
That is the same for all, whoever.
Because the fears are here, and they are mine. My fears. My mind.
Our fears. Our mind.

POWER

She has the power of a blizzard.
With her tears streaming down
In a river.
She is the beauty in a snowflake.
Fearing for the unforeseen moment,
Fearing to be fake, she shakes.

He has the power of a thunderstorm.
With his light from his eyes only seen
When it is both cold and warm.
He is the grace of a thunderclap.
Building up slowly,
Then giving in with a snap.

She has the power of a monsoon.
With her emotions forming like music,
Like a tune.
She is the soothing of a teardrop.
Passionate for her waves,
Never really wanting to give in and stop.

He has the power of a deluge,
But he is scared of what the sand might say,
So he is always seeking refuge.
He is the comfort of a mild breeze.
But he changes direction,
Always fearing to displease.

They have the powers of a wildfire.
They could let their emotions sing
Together in a momentous choir.
We have the powers of a wildfire.

But we control and hush our emotions
When we could sing loud instead of lying down.
Lying down on a pyre.

EMPTY

I knew what was going on.
I knew
Knew in my mind all along.

And it felt like a typhoon
Stirring up my heart
Ripping apart from the start.
I was left numb,
Empty,
Soon to be June, a girl of just twenty.

It would be easy to place the blame on her.
It was as if I was blind, everything in total blur.
It would be easy to say it was just the lust of weak mankind.
It was as if what we had was left behind.

At that point, I just wanted to stop breathing.
I just sat there staring –
Where was the caring?
It was empty,
It was numb.
No sleeping, a girl of just twenty.

Oh how I cried myself to sleep every day for months on end.
Crawled up, hunched, unable to comprehend.
Oh how I contemplated ending it all there, to descend.
All I wanted was to escape, to transcend.

And when I could see you repented
I felt guilty for not being more
For us being that to adore, for it all to be as before.
Understand how I was left empty

How I was left numb.
No sorrow was intended, but I was still a girl of just twenty.

I still wonder if I have forgiven you
Then it would be to ease my own pain.
I still wonder if I have healed
If I ever will be the same, sane.

So I forgive you
But so that I can live with myself.
I forgive you
So I can move on, let it be dawn.

Although I have never felt such aching.
I forgive myself for not being more,
For us not being easy to restore.
Because it was not my responsibility
This breaking.
It was you whose actions were to be answered for.

You should remember:
It was empty,
It was numb.
You should remember:
It was my destruction.
It ruined my constructions.

SHE JUST SAT THERE

She just sat there, crying.
Not hysterically crying, but silently.
Silently letting streams of water run down both of her cheeks.

She just sat there, complying.
Following instructions, doing what was told.
Submissively completing tasks for months and weeks.

She just sat there, trying.
Trying her best, her hardest, lifelessly.
Always listening, always staying quiet when someone speaks.

She just sat there, dying.
Slowly, withering away in obligations and concerns.
They were always above her, waiting, prepared with a poleaxe.

She just sat there, crying.
With a pounding head and tired eyes.
Silently letting streams of water run down both of her cheeks.

BLOCKAGE

I have a blockage
For intimacy.
I have a blockage
For opening.
I am so afraid of the power of my emotions
That I pause myself before I have even begun.

I am afraid of my capabilities,
Afraid of my force, so I barely speak.
I am afraid of my sensitive abilities,
Afraid of my strength. Some may think me weak.

Weak not because I am anxious
But because I silently wish to show.
I wish to remove my bond, my blockage
Because I hopingly wish to glow.

But I am afraid of what they might say
They who seek nothing more than those who shiver
Shiver in their presence, in their way
Hide behind the blockage, in the chaos river.

I have a blockage
For realising.
I have a blockage
For showing myself respect.
I am so afraid of showing my storms, my beautiful
Oceans
That I pause myself
Neglect believing to protect.

WANTING TO GET OUT

Aching
Pressing
Wanting to get out
Stinging
Longing
Wishing to shout

If we could just see how beautiful it would be,
When we first let out, give in.
Release and become free.

BREATHE

Never the ones to let go
The need for control is choking
We believe it to be strength
One day the lack of air will be exploding
The terror of this
Unspoken
I hope even the ever-improving images will one day accept being
Imperfect
Know we all have small cracks on the surface.
I hope the collective cries for help will one day console each other.
There is no need to hide or cover.
I hope even the toughest of thoughts will one day untighten.
See it is okay to be frightened.
I hope even the most heated of hearts will one day heal.
There is no more need to conceal.
I hope even the mistiest of minds will one day mend.
Never more to condescend.
For knowing we have to breathe will demolish the boding.
No unspoken.
Only flowing.
Growing.

CALMING

If we could just see how
Calming it could be.
If we could just hear
How reassuring it is out here.

The earth is rumbling
Because it is tired of our correct noise.
The earth is demanding silence
It wants us to learn about the poise.

Out here it would be so soothing
If we would just give in
Let it pour
Let it rain
Release our pain
Give what our heart calls for.

Will we ever understand?
The balance
The poise.
The earth is demanding it nevertheless
It wants our emotions and internal wishes to coalesce.

Swords

ALL THREE EYES

People do not see
People do not hear
People fear feeling free
Because it is heavy.

People fear to be carefree
People fear to show their weaknesses.
People seek shielding the savagery they see
Because all else is wearisome.

People seek to be blind
People bind their own ties.
People fear climbing out of what creates being confined.
Because all else is thought to be demise.

People climb away from their passions
People dread their own sunrise.
People pour silencing poison onto their poetic potentials
Because rising demands the removal of disguise.

But what if we tried giving ourselves the freedom
The freedom to humanise.
It seems we have completely lost our colourful compassion
We should meet each other more often with compromise.

So what if we tried giving ourselves the liberty.
The liberty to become each other's allies,
To abolish our bigoted binds.
What if we tried to see with all three eyes?

THE SUPREMACY OF *NORMALITY*

Have you ever heard about the greatest minds?
About how they were destroyed by the insanity that lingers?
The ones who see clearly the shapes in clandestine.
The only ones who notice the hidden figures.

They hide themselves from the common world.
Hide themselves from the words that belong to this world.
They stay in the shadows, in their own creations.
Beneath, lurking – frightened and curled.

Frightened of the power of judgment
That is in all worldly men's possession.
Frightened of the supremacy of normality,
So they flee in the fear of censured expression.

They flee in the fear of having wiped away their curves.
Flee in the fear of having to be square.
Do you not notice how they suffer?
Try to notice with all three eyes open, be aware.

Be aware of the quelling cages.
Be aware of the clout of blinds.
Because the true insanity that lingers
Is the one that suppresses the greatest minds.

PERFECT

We build the materials that build buildings
And the materials that are built to build buildings
Do not build themselves.

We cut, adjust, and deprive ourselves.
We judge, compare and act all tough.
What is the point when we are afraid of being ourselves?
What is the point of flawless when unflawed is never enough?
It has to be perfect
Perfect.

Take it from someone who has tried fitting into other people's standards.
Starving is not the same as perseverance.
Oh wait, where are my manners?!
Sure, just judge me for my appearance.
Am I perfect yet?
Perfect.

Stop leaving yourself behind.
Because you are the only one who will follow you to the end.
The *perfect* shape is not something to be outlined.
You will just end up playing pretend.
But it has to be perfect
Perfect.

Being hungry for other people's approval is not worth starving for.
Fighting for the perfect body is like going into cold war.
Our weapons are our minds, our battleground are ourselves.
So save yourself before you kill yourself.
It does not have to be perfect
Imperfect.

OTHER'S SIGHT

Sky eyes
It was just a dream.
At times it felt so much more than just a dream.
A dream of those
Sky eyes.
A dream of those
Sapphire ties.

But alas the dream was mine
And at times I feared that it was only mine.
Because the ways were shut.
Shut for your affection.
Doors closed.
Mirrors showing no more than my own complexion.

I know that you did not *not* choose me.
I know what you felt, what we felt.
But I also know why it could not last.
Darling, we stood no chance against the world's demanding welt.
Neither of us had the strength to endure.
To beat back with power, with might.
We stood no chance against the people's expectations.
Stood no chance against their strains so tight.

And so, it was just a dream
A dream of mine, a dream of yours.
But we both know dreams are made for the moonlight.
Not for us, nor for the sun, and not for others' sight.

But what pity
That their eyes should be allowed to judge.
What pity
That their eyes should be allowed to hush our touch.

SIDELINE

I was standing on the sideline,
But your words made me feel like swords swinging at me on the battleground.
Did you stop to think about how it would affect me?
How your disputes would jump at me, rebound.

It makes me angry you had me crying on my day.
Even though I have had twenty others to prepare.
You had people talking, going in circles after the party had ended.
All because you felt the need to go into warfare.

I knew I had to pull myself together.
Maybe I should even have acted stronger.
I keep my mouth shut, buried my fury.
But now I cannot keep quiet about this any longer.

You acted like a child.
It was impossible for you to see the other side.
You affected the world around you.
All because you had too much vehemence, confusing it with pride.

Wipe away the drops, take a deep breath.
Your behavior was rotten, your words were poor.
I thought more of you, thought you were above this.
Though I never expected you to have grandeur.

It sent me back to that one day,
When you were standing above me, scolding.
A child with no force, no power.
Desperate, for her defence to start unfolding.

It never did though,
The defence never came.

I felt abandoned in my feelings, immobilized.
Your sight was penetrating, your words hit with perfect aim.

In reality I was used to it, I had seen it before.
Your force was grand, always trying to be above her.
Do you know she tries her best, her hardest?
But your last inch of respect has been washed off, into total blur.

I knew I would see it again
I knew it ran in your veins, in our bloodline.
I suppose I was always your unfortunate casualty
Never truly safe standing on the sideline.

THE WORST SIGHT

Do you know what the worst sight is?
Do you realize what the darkest light is?

Silence has us standing in a corner.
Standing with walls on all sides.
Silence has us lying on a platter.
It forces us to split ourselves, divide.

Because the mind is lost when the heart is shushed.
The mind is drifting when the thoughts are waved away.
The heart is adrift when the bumps are unaccepted, unrecognized.
The heart is lost when the feelings are rejected, despised.

It can be others' doing.
It can be our own.
But it is mostly our own rejection, our own refutation,
Our own denial, which leaves us feeling alone.

Stillness has us sitting in the dark
Sitting with our eyes looking upwards, supine;
Stillness has us climbing away from what our soul needs;
It forces us to break our wishes, confine.

Because the heart is lost when the mind is held down.
The heart is rootless when our possibilities are waved away.
The mind is rootless when the desires are unseen, unrealized.
The mind is lost when passion and hopes are not unionised.

It can be others' doing,
It can be our own.
Mostly it is our own depriving nature, our own extermination,
Our own rejection of our motivating prospects, which leaves us feeling alone.

So, do you now realize what the worst sight is?
To see someone you love losing their mind.
Lose their mind by their own doing, their own depriving thoughts.
Because they kept shushing and waving away their otherwise beautiful crazy knots.

So, do you now see what the darkest light is?
To see someone, leave their heart behind.
Leave their heart because they forgot, because they did not fight feeling astray.
Because they kept sitting still, kept looking away.

IT RAN RED

It ran red
My innocence
My youth
My inexperience.
It ran red.

I have never spoken about it.
I do not think I ever want to speak about it.
Why? Shame? Myself to blame?

I went there
With drunk consent,
Thought it would be different.
This was not my intent.

When is it over?
Is it soon to be over?

And when I was crawling home
Shaking,
Ripped trousers dirty from the cold ground,
Aching,
A dream of escape was just that:
A dream.
All I could think of was my fright,
A grip that was so tight.

When is it over?
Is it soon to be over?

And after?
Well I walked out

Fearing to wake him
Cautiously taking the dark route.
I couldn't sit,
The pain too excruciating.
Everything was misfit,
The aching too pulsating.

Scream and I
Quiet
Turned me around
Again
Again
Again
Again
The pain
Dear Gods, the pain.

When is it over?
Is it soon to be over?

Not a word
I was frozen, stunned.
Waiting for it to be done
Held down, and?
Still not a word,
Run.

When is it over?
Is it soon to be over?

And when it was
Finally over
The same question filled my mind.
He is pressing my head against the pillow.
Can this really be the true nature of mankind?

And when it was
Finally over
The sour pill I had to swallow
To kill what might had been made.
The blood in the shower, how I felt hollow.

But am I to blame myself,
For this pain I could feel for weeks after?
Please go no faster.
Am I to blame myself?
For this shame, I can feel for years later.
Please let me forget this violator.
Am I to blame myself
For the smile I had before I walked through that door?
Am I the whore?
Am I to blame myself?
For my naive thinking?
For what if someone sees me on my way home,
Limping?
Am I to blame myself?
For my shame.
Pain.

No,
But it still ran red.

ENDURE, FIGHT

Let me tell you a story of fearing and enduring
When I started eating again at a time when I wanted to throw up.
Let me tell you a story of healing and maturing
When I hid away the scale and threw out the measuring cup.

Because after being scarred for life
I forced myself to try to love again.
I went out knowing the world held the coldest and darkest of mankind
After experiencing tearing and the foulest of pain.

Let me tell you a story of emotional ripping
A time of mental strife, screams, and cloudiness.
Let me tell you how I continued to stitch and sew
How I fought to quiet the loudness.

Because I pulled myself together when I was at my worst
I rode out the cries and terror locked in my room.
I fought for my mind when I feared the worst
When it felt like the world was at its doom.

And what did you do
When you were afraid
When you hid in your room, frightened for the world
Exploding every time someone mentioned pulling down your barricade?

What did you do?
When we were there to help you save you
When we over and over again fought for your life.
Yet only few understand how we tried to pull you through.

But you did nothing
Did you not want to?

Start doing something.
The darkest of days too.

But you did nothing
Did you not want to fight for yourself?
But will you soon start doing something?
The foulest of nights as well.

I know you can do something
I know you can fight for your life
I know you can fight for the ending of your troubles
Even when it feels the world is coming at you with a knife.

JUST BEFORE

Just before I fall
I am feeling so small
Like a leaf that crumbles
Breaking into pieces,
Wanting to steal others' breathing sources.
Getting smaller and smaller,
Becoming a thief.
I ask myself
What is the point of this grief?

Okay,
This is too depressing.
Just pull yourself together.

I am feeling so small,
Like a fly on the wall,
Observing.
Watching as I see my life fall,
Seemingly because the life I built was surrounded by the wrong walls.
These are the scars that are not patchable.
These are the scars that will always stay visible.

I am feeling kind of small
Without the real power,
The power to steer.
The power to decide for me, for others, for the better.
Without the power to wipe my mind clear.

Okay,
This is too depressing.
Just pull yourself together.

I am feeling so small.
But I am getting bigger,
Should I dare wish; even stronger?
Because I might think my strength is getting thicker.

When I act
The decisions are getting wider
Wider with knowledge,
Wider with comprehensions.

When I act
My mind is turning into a fighter.
With the strength of a rebel,
Would I even dare say – becoming mightier?

I am feeling so small.
But for the thousandth time,
I pull myself up.
Climbing the walls, cleaning my wounds,
Wiping my tears, accepting my moons.
And when I am feeling this small
And I think to myself, what is the point?
I dare say: Keep fighting and stop yourself before the last fall.
And after before
I stop feeling this small.

Tears

LISTEN

Let us release one another.
One way or another.
Listen as we plea:
We want to break free!

There is running, there is shunning
But there is no hiding.

We cannot escape, we cannot change shape.
There is no abiding.

So let us release one another.
One way or another.
Listen as we release.
Here it comes: We cease!

OVERWHELMING

It is an overwhelming feeling
When you give in.
It is an overwhelming feeling
When you release, *sin*.

Because we are taught that showing is sinning.
We are taught to cover, create a layer of thinning.
Because covering is said to protect,
When in reality not showing is just a way of neglect.

It is an overwhelming feeling
When you put your emotions on display for the world to see.
It is an overwhelming feeling
When you express what you could justly be.

Because we are taught that displaying is ill set.
That when we are not hiding it is ill met.
Because we are taught that hiding is better than to share,
When in reality it is just inconvenient for those who want us to be square.

IT TOOK LONG TO GET HERE

I have been laughed at
Haven't we all
I have been yelled at
Been divided into two halves

I have been rejected
Slapped
Shut down, discriminated.

I have been touched
Crapped
Held down, humiliated.

I will forever carry the shame.
Forever remember the pain.

I have been deceived
Had my heart broken
By people who were supposed to care for me.
I have grieved
Apologies left unspoken
People I trusted brought me down to my knees.

I will forever carry the maim.
Forever remember their names.

I have been loved
I have caused tears
I have caused laughter
I have had my fears
My eyes may look strong
Do not forget, it took long to get here.
You may think I am always smiling.
That is only because you cannot see me lean on a spear.

WRITTEN IN SAND

What is written in stone?
Carved
There forever
Signs standing side by side
Together.
Not ours

What is written in bone?
Marked
Everlasting
Adding an accessory
To repent collapsing.
Not ours

What is written in skin, in our hands?
Scarred
Stretched duration
Never forever, new natural covering with
White enation.
Not ours

What is written in sand?
Touched with a finger
Thought it was conjoint, ready to embrace.
Does it matter how deep down we dug?
Nature erase, for time leaves little trace.
Ours

BUT I AM SAYING IT OUT LOUD

I am saying it out loud
I am getting my wings now
But they are still wet from being submerged under water.
Dripping
When I turn my head and look at them.
I do not want to participate in this anymore, this
Slaughter.

I am saying it out loud
And it breaks the walls.
I feel the ending of killing of my feelings.
Releasing
As I feel the water pressing against my barrier.
Pressing against, wanting to break free.
I am kneeling.

I am saying it out loud
I am giving in, kneeling and
Bending.
I have felt my knees sinking for too long now.
Sinking into my emotions, into
Quicksand.

I am saying it out loud.
I admit it, I acknowledge it.
Forgiving
Myself for what I feel,
For my waters.
I am moonlit.

I am saying it out loud.
Because I can see what I feel now, it is all clear, it is
Illuminated.
My wings show because I admit it.
Even though they are still wet, they are not submerged any longer.
They fit, it fits.

TRANQUILLITY

The yelling world outside is quiet compared to my mind.
Because my head is filled with noiseless words screaming for salvation.
Only the storms in the sky can calm down my devouring thoughts.
I suppose thunder has a skill for tranquil creation.

Maybe my mind *is* different, maybe my emotions *are* stronger.
The creation of the mind must have been a complicated task.
Others might think I am wrong for not hiding my feelings
But I refuse to keep wearing this gray mask.

Let them know that emotions are in colors.
Not in black and white.
People think everything has to be so clean, so discreet.
How do they not see the beauty in this unstable colorful sight?

WHAT DO I WANT?

What
Do we
Want?
What do we want?
What do I want?

Do I want to think about the world's problems and measures?
Do I want to fall in the wind and look endlessly for the world's treasures?
Do I want to see the earth fall and the air perish?
Do I want to question myself and be fairish?
Do I want to be daunted?
Is this what I wanted?

Do I want to question myself and my decisions?
Do I want continually to look for answers and fall into collisions?
Do I want to doubt my decisions and forget the answers?
Fall through the glass while looking for standards.
Dive into water, to be at empty sea.
Looking for answers inside me.

Do I want to disappoint?
Do I want to fail?
Do I want to yield to the world?
Do I want to pressure myself? To hale?
Do I want to weep?
Do I want my heart to seep?
Or do I want something else?
Do I want something else?

Do I want to follow, with no mind or soul of my own?
Do I want hunger to be my force or do I want force to be my clone?
Do I want sorrow to fill?

Do I want confusion to kill?

Do I want tears? Do I want fake smiles?
Do I want mistakes to steer, to steer thousands of miles?
Do I want the world to fall at my feet? Or do I just want to fall to the earth?
Do I want to disappear or just slowly be less worth?

Do I want more? Do I want less?
Do I want materials, do I want to possess?
Do I want to follow the rules?
Do I want several tools,
Tools to build walls, materials to shape my physique?
Do I want to be sorry? Do I want to be weak?

Do I want to have
More than others or do I want to halve?
Do I want to take from people,
Feeling empty without having the power to climb the steeple?
Do I want to fall behind,
Feeling like my destiny is twined
With terrible endings and risky pretending?
Or do I want something else?
Do I want something else?

What do I want?

I want to listen to the wind, listen to the birds.
I want to feel earth beneath my feet, and I want to read kind words.
I want to sing, and I want to feel the cold wind around me.
I want to cook, to eat and be truly free.
I want to see love and I want to see wishes.
To see compassion and feel the precious kisses.
Without shame. Without humiliation.
Without sorrow and cruel negation.

I want to believe in wonder and creation. I want to believe in miracles and luck.
I want to feel what is right. I want to do what feels true without being stuck.

I want to wonder. I want to create.
I want to be honest and I want my heart to relate.
Relate to others. Possess compassion,
Be strong and have passion.
I want to be calm
Without hiding feelings and then give up like a bomb.
I want to give.
I want to live.
I want to be free.
I want to be me.

EQUILIBRIUM

It is a feeling,
This equilibrium.
It is hard to explain.
It is a feeling,
This awaited healing.
It is difficult to contain.

But mother, I hope that you are proud of me.
Because I have learned to live, with the evil words by the world who speak.
And father, I hope that you are proud of me.
Because I have learned to fight for what I believe in and thus learned what I am supposed to teach.
And friend, I hope that you are proud of me.
Because I have learned to thrive, in a world that crumbles.
I have learned to be me, to get up, and to look the world in the eye every time I tumble.

It is a feeling,
A feeling of equilibrium.
It is hard to explain.
But I hope that you are proud.
Because it is a feeling in me.
A feeling of equilibrium.
A feeling of being unbound.

SUNDIAL AND DEFILE

An acknowledgment of the resolution empowered

I might leave, but I will never forget this place.
I will look back once in a while.
There was a certain grace about this space.
It made me, by sundial and defile:
Because time was slow, and it showed.
The marks formed here I will bring with me wherever I go.
I know it cannot be left behind.
It was what made me grow.

NOTES

The title of this poetry collection, *Blizzards, Swords & Tears,* is inspired by the phrase "Blood, sweat, and tears" popularized by the late prime minister of the United Kingdom Winston Churchill. Churchill used the line "I have nothing to offer but blood, toil, tears, and sweat" in a speech from 1940. The phrase may date back from various translations of the Bible mentioning Jesus who "Bathed in his own blood, sweat, and tears."

The opening poem 'Hope for change' was created using the cut-up technique, also known as *découpé,* by using an issue of the *MoMa Magazine* from April 2015 from the Museum of Modern Art in New York City.

The words "chaos river" in the fourth stanza of the poem 'Blockage' was inspired by John Milton's epic poem *Paradise Lost.* The words 'chaos river' are an interpretation of the mental space one might reside when fearing another's judging words, and when having certain blocked emotions. These entities in the fourth stanza are hence linked to the demons in Milton's poem.

The title and concept of the poem 'All three eyes' are inspired by the notion of having Chakras found in Tantra, various ancient meditation practices, and the esoteric or inner traditions of Hinduism and Buddhism. Specifically, the poem and its title point to Ajna, also known as the Third-Eye Chakra.

The poem 'The supremacy of *normality*' was inspired by Allen Ginsberg's poem 'Howl' from 1956. The words 'the greatest mind' in line one was triggered by the very first part of the first line of Ginsberg's poem; "I saw the best minds of my generation destroyed by madness,[…]", as well as of the repeating use of the noun "Minds".

ACKNOWLEDGMENTS

Sincere gratitude to the editors and publishers of this poetry collection who helped turn this dream of being published into reality.
Dr Todd Swift, for believing in this collection, even written by a newly birthed and inexperienced poet, from the very beginning. Dr Alex Wylie, for being patient with my grammatical errors as a non-native English speaker. Edwin Smet, for bringing my wishes and ideas for the covers visual to life in such a beautiful way, and everyone else at Eyewear Publishing involved in the process of this publication.

*

All those in middle school who *commented* on my weirdness. Your *constructive* criticism inspired me to love myself no matter what.
The drunken soul whose actions became a catalyst for pain, healing, and eventually creative creation.
Sima, for lighting the spark for my love for English literature and the English language.
Professor Lock, for teaching me everything useful technically I know about writing poetry and all of my other teachers at Copenhagen University.
To my friends at University – Spanish O.
Magnus, for always reminding me of my Danish grammatical errors in High School – Biffelmobd.
My sweet Darling Julie, who for many years has listened to my endless creative outburst, read my early (slightly terrible) literary works, and who despite my excessive love for floral and color has stood by my side as a contrast made of angelic sarcasm. You have been

the greatest friend an aspiring writer and poet could have dreamt for in her young adulthood – Always and forever.

Emma, my absolute favorite person in London.

Sofie, for being my partner in crime since the age of 6 and sister to the end of our days – We are opposites yet the very same.

Louise, and all my other friends from my childhood town with who much time in nature and the city was spent.

My Guides – thank you for your protection.

My nephews Marius and Julius, for being like little brothers to me.

My Goddaughters Estella and Luisa, who has made me realize what truly matters; family.

Tatiana, for becoming my sister through a bond of love and for showing me that wonderful and beautiful people are found all over the world.

My siblings, who have raised me along with my parents and always inspired me in my creative processes.

Anne, for showing me what a fierce woman looks like.

Martin, for giving me endless love and support in whatever endeavor I chose to embark on.

Emiel, for being one of, if not the biggest, artistic inspirations in my life.

My father, who showed me the reality of being human, and that helping and giving advice to those you care for is the greatest virtue one can wish to learn.

My mother, whose endless love and overcoming of unimaginable experiences has shown me what true strength is made of. You are my root that keeps me grounded – Thank you.